# Family in Islam

*Quranic Verses and Sayings from the 14 Ma'soomeen*

Islām places great emphasis on the importance of family. A prospering society is made up of healthy families, which are the essence of a society. The ideal Islāmic family is one with a warm, nurturing atmosphere whose positive effects are manifest in everyone, especially the children. In fact, the beneficial effects of a positive family environment transcend beyond the household, and its blessings are palpable within the society at large.

وَ بِالْوَالِدَينِ إِحْسَانًا

And be good and kind to your parents.

Sūrah al-Baqarah, Verse 83

There was once a man who had just become a Muslim! Because he was new to Islam, he wanted to make sure that he was living his life in a way where Allah would be happy with him. He was the only one in his family who had become a Muslim, so he wondered, *if I am a Muslim and my parents are not Muslim, should I stay away from them? Should I refuse to help them?*

He decided to seek an answer for his question from the wisest person of his time: Imam Sadiq (a). After exchanging salaams, he asked the Imam (a), "my dear mother is very old and she lost her sight. Can I help her and my father even though they are not Muslim? How should I treat them?"

"Of course you should help them!" replied the Imam (a). "In fact, you should be more kind and loving than ever before, especially to your mother since she has lost her sight."

After hearing this, the man felt relieved. He thanked the Imam (a) and made his way back home. As soon as he saw his mother, he began to treat her better than ever before. He cooked for her, fed her, washed her clothes, and kept the house nice and tidy. He showed both of his parents a lot of love and care.

His mother was surprised. She was not used to her son being this kind to her. One day, she asked, "my dear son, when you used to follow our religion, you never treated me this well. Now that you follow Islam, why do you show me so much more love?"

Her son smiled and replied, "my Imam taught me that Muslims should have good behavior and be especially kind and loving toward their parents."

She paused for a moment and asked, "Can I please meet your Imam?"

"Of course! I would love to introduce you to him!" he answered.

The next day, he took his mother to visit the Imam (a). They had a conversation about some of the beautiful teachings of Islam, and she immediately fell in love with it. When she returned home, she couldn't stop thinking about what she had learned. She was most surprised by how Islam was so different to the rumors she had heard. She regretted having jumped to conclusions in the past. "Next time I hear about something, I'll be sure to research more," she promised herself. Day by day, she began to learn more and reflect more until one day, she, too, decided to become Muslim!

Uṣūl al-Kāfī, Chapter on Parents, Ḥadīth #11

مَنْ أَرْضَى وَالِدَيْهِ فَقَدْ أَرْضَى الله

**Prophet Muhammad (s):**
Whoever makes his mother and father happy has indeed made Allah happy.

Kanz ul-Ummāl, Vol 12

وَ شَاوِرْهُمْ فِي الْأَمْرِ

And seek advice for important matters in your life.

Sūrah Āl-ʿImrān, Verse 159

One night, a man was fast asleep after a long day of work. In his dream, an angel came to him and said, "you will live half of your life while you are rich and comfortable, and you will live the other half of your life while you are poor and troubled. Which half do you want to live first?"

He thought for a moment but still felt unsure. "I need to ask my wife for advice before making a decision," he told the angel. You see, he and his wife would always consult each other before making important decisions.

The next morning, he told his wife about the dream. "Which one do you think I should choose first?" he asked her. She suggested that he ask Allah for the easy part of life to come first. He agreed and took her advice.

From that day forward, the man and his wife lived a rich and comfortable life for many years, and they would always thank Allah for giving them so many blessings! They even decided to share their wealth with the poor.

As the good times were coming to an end, the same angel came back to his dream and said, "the time to live in comfort is almost over, but since you and your wife were thankful and generous, Allah wants you to also live the second half of your life in comfort and wealth also!"

The man woke up and rushed to share the good news with his wife. They were both filled with joy, and would go on to thank Allah and help the poor more than ever before. He turned to his wife and thanked her for giving him such good advice.

Biḥār ul-Anwār, Vol. 68, Page 55

لا نَدِمَ مَنِ اسْتَشَارَ

**Prophet Muhammad (s):**
There is no regret for the one who asks for advice [from the right people].

Biḥār ul-Anwār, Vol. 75, P. 83

لَا تَتَّخِذُوا بِطَانَةً مِّنْ دُونِكُمْ

Do not tell your secrets to just anyone.

Sūrah Āl-ʿImrān, Verse 118

A man was once feeling very worried and stressed about his problems, so he went to Imam Sadiq (a) to tell him all about them.

The Imam (a) listened carefully and tried to put himself in the man's shoes. He lifted his hands up and prayed, "may Allah remove all of your hardships!" The Imam (a) then comforted the man and gave him enough money to help him fix his problems.

*Whenever I need help, the Imam always gives me more than I could imagine,* the man thought. *His prayers alone would have been plenty!*

As he was leaving, the Imam (a) gave him a piece of advice. "Be careful not to tell your secrets to just anybody," he said. "When people hear about your problems, they might lose respect for you. Also, not everyone knows how to give good advice."

The man thanked the Imam (a) and decided to be more careful about sharing his problems with others. As he walked away, he thought to himself, *thank God I have someone like the Imam to turn to for advice!*

Biḥār ul-Anwār, Vol. 47, P. 34

إِحْفَظْ لِسَانَكَ تَعِزَّ

**Imam Musa al-Kadhim (a):**
If you watch what you say, you will have more honor and respect.

Biḥār ul-Anwār, Vol. 75, P. 83

وَ قُل لِّعِبَادِى يَقُولُوا الَّتِى هِيَ أَحْسَنُ

Tell My servants to speak in the best way.

Sūrah al-Isrāʾ, Verse 53

There was once a man who loved Imam Sadiq (a) very much and would visit him quite often.

One night while the man was having a chat with his mother, the conversation turned into an argument. In anger, he began to raise his voice and say cruel things.

Early the next morning, he went to the masjid for prayer. After he finished praying, he got up to greet the Imam (a). But before he could say anything, the Imam (a) asked, "Why did you speak harshly with your mother last night?"

Surprised that the Imam (a) knew about it, he hung his head in shame. The Imam (a) continued, "Be careful with how you speak to others, especially your mother. She is the one who brought you into this world, fed you when you were hungry, and cradled you in her arms." The Imam (a) then reminded him to always speak nicely to people, especially parents and elders.

The man took this advice seriously. As soon as he reached home, he apologized to his mother, kissed her hand, and asked her for forgiveness.

Biḥār ul-Anwār, Vol. 47, P. 72

أَجْمِلُوا فِي الْخِطَابِ تَسْمَعُوا جَمِيْلَ الْجَوَابِ

Imam Ali (a):
Speak to others nicely, and you will also hear a nice reply from them.

Ghurar al-Ḥikam, P. 436

وَ تَعَاوَنُوا عَلَى الْبِرِّ وَ التَّقْوَى

And help each other be good and God-conscious.

Sūrah al-Māʾidah, Verse 2

One summer afternoon, the Prophet (s) decided to go on a trip with three of his friends. On the way, they stopped outside town to pray and have lunch. After prayer, they decided to each take a task to prepare lunch.

"I will go get the meat!" one person volunteered.

"I will cook the meat!" another offered.

"Leave it to me to set the tablecloth!" said the third.

"And I will gather the firewood," volunteered the Prophet (s).

All three men said, "O Prophet of Allah! Please sit down and rest. Give us the honor of preparing the food for you!"

The Prophet (s) thanked them for their kindness and said, "I'm sure that you can handle it on your own, but I also want to help. Allah does not like it when a group travels together and someone does not pitch in to help with the work."

He then set out to collect firewood. Within the hour, they were all gathered around the tablecloth enjoying a delicious meal together.

Biḥār ul-Anwār, Vol. 5

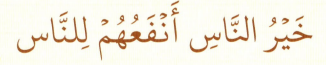

خَيْرُ النَّاسِ أَنْفَعُهُمْ لِلنَّاس

**Prophet Muhammad (s):**
The best people are those who are most helpful to others.

Kanz ul-Ummāl, Vol.1, P.142

# QUIZ YOURSELF!

1. When a new Muslim asked for advice about how to treat his non-Muslim mother, he was told to _____.
a. find a new place to live.
b. treat her with even more kindness.
c. treat her in a harsh way so that she can learn a lesson.

2. According to the Prophet (s), if you ask the right people advice for right people, you will not be _____.
a. worried
b. regretful
c. angry

3. Imam Sadiq (a) teaches us that whenever we have a problem and need to ask for help, we should _____.
a. be sure to tell everyone about our problems; the more the merrier.
b. not ask for help from anyone and always keep our secrets to ourselves.
c. ask for advice from people we trust.

4. We should speak kindly to everyone, especially our _____.
a. parents
b. teachers
c. friends

5. According to the Prophet (s), Allah likes it when _____.
a. one person volunteers to do all of the work.
b. nobody does the work.
c. Muslims work together as a team.

6. Name three ways you can respect your parents.

7. Name three people whom you can go to for advice.

EMAIL YOUR ANSWERS TO QUIZZES@KISAKIDS.ORG, AND WE WILL SEND YOU A CERTIFICATE!